The Adventures of Scuba Jack
Copyright 2020 by Beth Costanzo
All rights reserved

Grizzly bears are powerful, top-of-the-food-chain predators found in North America and Canada. The grizzly bear is a big, typically brown bear that weighs from 300 to 1,500 pounds and stands up to 8 feet tall!

Male grizzly bears can be twice the size of female grizzly bears. A baby grizzly bear is called a cub. It can weigh 200 pounds by the time it's one year old. Even though grizzly bears are massive animals, they can still run up to 35 miles per hour. Their natural behavior is to avoid and not pick fights with others. But, it will defend itself if needed!

Most people think that these bears can only be brown, but they can range from black, blonde, silver and even white. The tip of their fur can be a different color, which gives them a "grizzled" look, meaning grey-tipped hair. Grizzly bears look different from other bears because they have long curved claws, and humped shoulders that give them power to dig in the ground and rip apart dead logs to find food.

Grizzly bears are omnivores, which means they eat plants and animals, and they find their food with their great sense of smell. They like to eat berries, fish, rodents, roots, moths, and small animals. Sometimes they will eat deer and elk, but they will usually eat anything that is available.

In the late summer and fall, grizzly bears spend a lot of time looking for food and eating it. This extra food adds an extra layer of fat to its body so it can live in its den for four to seven months during the coldest weather. This is called "Hibernation." Grizzly bears don't eat or drink throughout this entire hibernation period.

Most of the time, grizzly bears live alone. The biggest gathering is during the salmon run in Alaska. When the salmon migrate upstream for the summer, grizzly bears gather to catch their fish. The largest bears get the first catch!

Grizzly Bear Activities

Trace then rewrite the phrase below.

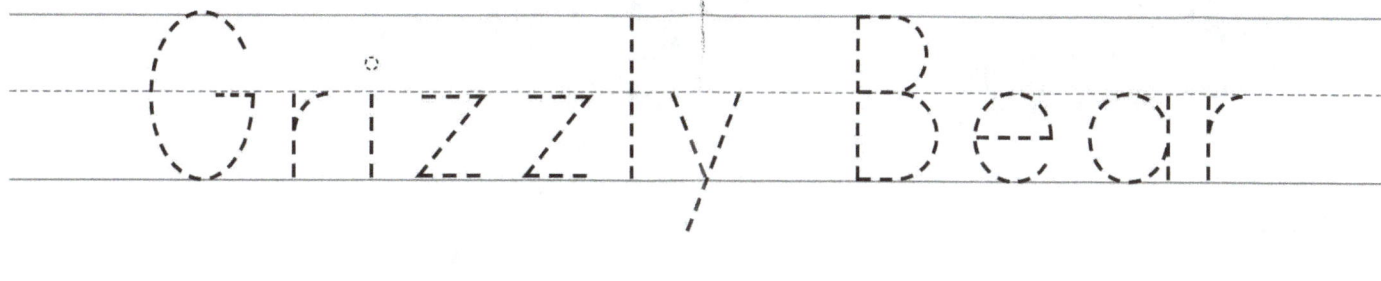

BODY PARTS

Back
Fur
Tail
Ears
Head
Eyes
Nose
Mouth
Paw
Claws
Legs

GRIZZY BEAR

Count the grizzly bears then circle the answer.

4   5   6    7   8   9

8   9   10    7   6   8

COUNT AND WRITE

 =	 =	 =	 =

COUNT AND TRACE THE MISSING NUMBERS

1	2	3	4	5
6	7	8	9	10
11	12	13	14	15
16	17	18	19	20
21	22	23	24	25
26	27	28	29	30

COUNT AND GRAPH

CONNECT THE DOTS

WORD SEARCH

and circle the words listed below.

H	F	C	H	B	B	C	L	C	U	C	G	O	I
D	Z	Y	O	U	R	I	Y	W	S	D	E	E	R
F	G	E	U	V	U	K	O	S	D	E	K	K	D
U	P	J	K	B	O	F	J	E	F	C	K	B	T
R	A	H	Q	R	U	G	K	L	I	J	I	E	W
E	M	Y	F	O	R	D	U	K	S	V	M	R	G
I	O	J	J	D	I	A	U	H	H	X	C	R	H
I	T	W	U	E	B	E	A	R	D	R	U	I	K
S	H	I	E	N	P	U	O	H	O	A	B	E	M
N	S	N	U	T	R	M	Y	E	B	O	D	S	H
A	I	V	Y	S	V	I	M	H	X	S	M	G	H
D	M	P	A	W	S	M	G	R	I	Z	Z	L	Y
M	C	N	A	V	I	M	M	Z	A	M	T	H	B
B	Y	Y	C	M	K	S	I	D	P	D	Z	X	C

Deer   Moths   Cub   Berries   Paws

~~Bear~~   Rodents   Fish   Fur   Elk

BABY ANIMAL

A baby bear is called a cub

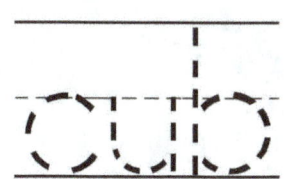

Count and write the number of cubs below.

Color the bear

LABEL THEM

FISH   **CUB**   **SUN**

TREE   **BEAR**   **GRASS**

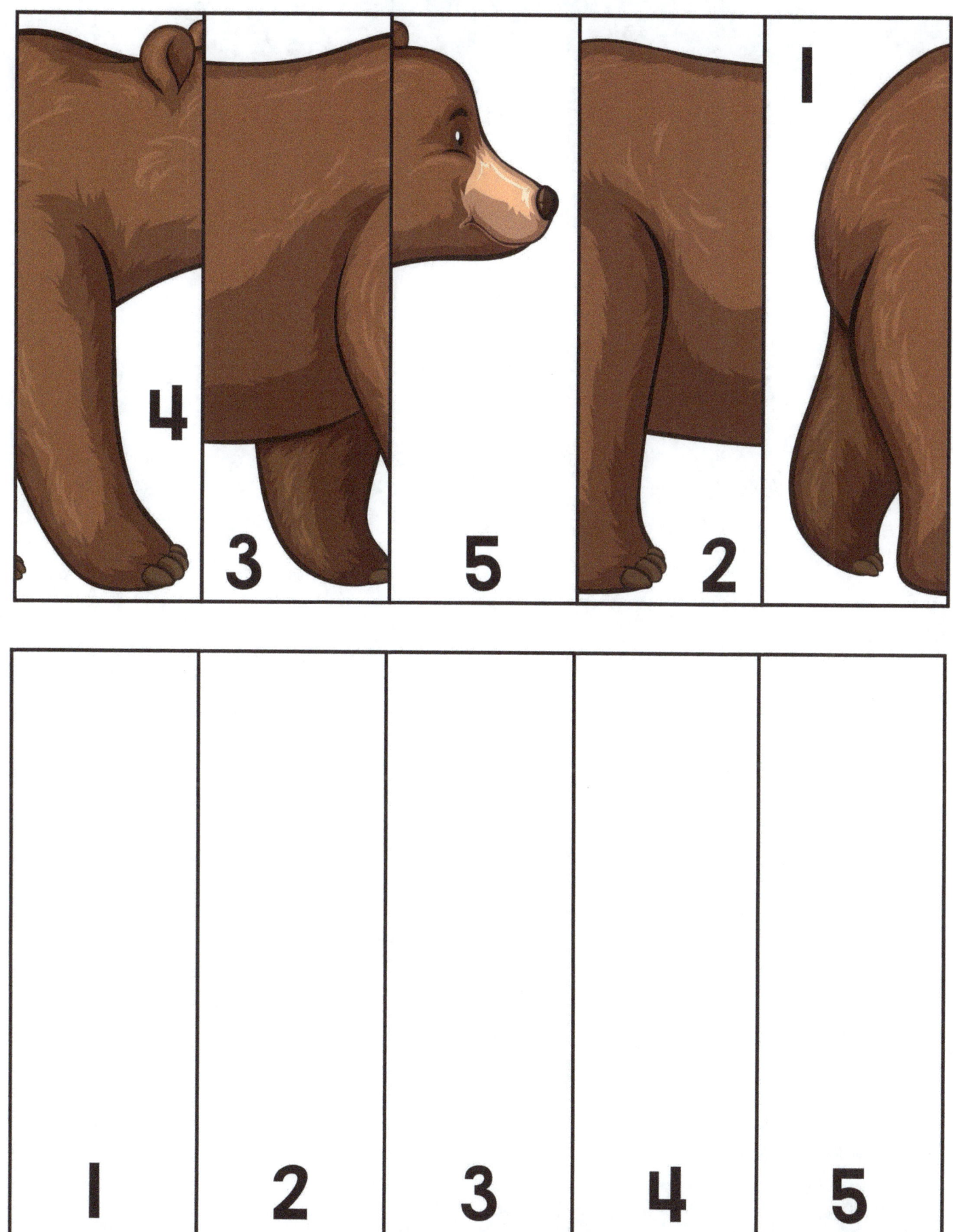

COLOR IT

Grizzly Bear Craft

1- Cut out the Grizzly bear Parts
2- Glue the head to the body
3- Glue the back legs to the body
4- Color your Grizzly Bear!

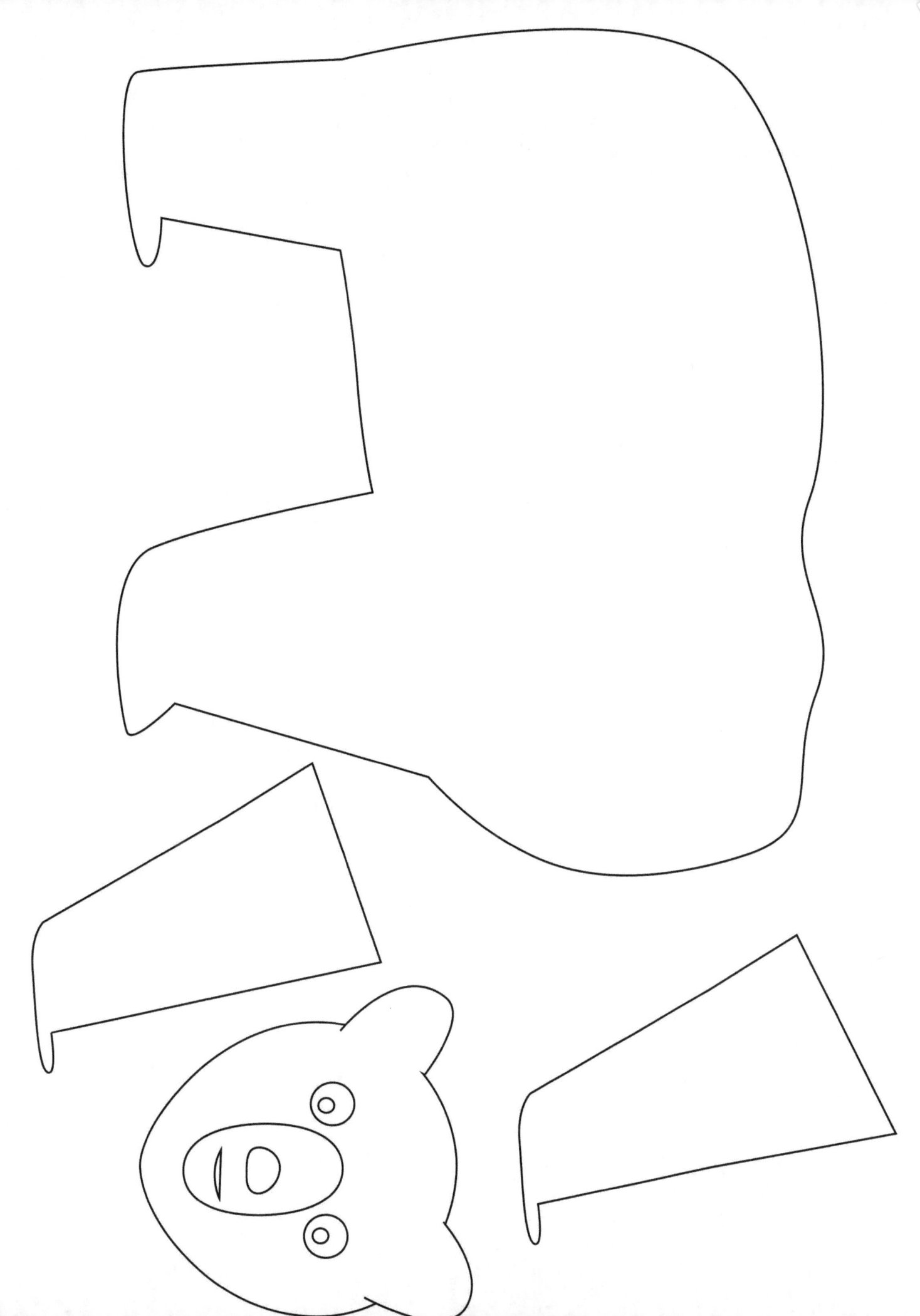

Visit us at:

www.adventuresofscubajack.com

www.ingramcontent.com/pod-product-compliance
Lightning Source LLC
Chambersburg PA
CBHW060429010526
44118CB00017B/2417